SLENDER HUMAN WEIGHT

ESSENTIAL POETS SERIES 168

Canada Council
for the Arts

Conseil des Arts
du Canada

Guernica Editions Inc. acknowledges the support of
the Canada Council for the Arts.

SUE CHENETTE

SLENDER HUMAN

WEIGHT

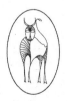

GUERNICA
TORONTO — BUFFALO — CHICAGO — LANCASTER (U.K.)
2009

Elana Wolff, editor
Guernica Editions Inc.
P.O. Box 117, Station P, Toronto (ON), Canada M5S 2S6
2250 Military Road, Tonawanda, N.Y. 14150-6000 U.S.A.

Distributors:
University of Toronto Press Distribution,
5201 Dufferin Street, Toronto (ON), Canada M3H 5T8
Gazelle Book Services, White Cross Mills, High Town, Lancaster LA1 4XS U.K.
Independent Publishers Group,
814 N. Franklin Street, Chicago, Il. 60610 U.S.A.

First edition.
Printed in Canada.

Legal Deposit – Fourth Quarter
Library of Congress Catalog Card Number: 2009938412
Library and Archives Canada Cataloguing in Publication
Chenette, Sue
Slender human weight / Sue Chenette.
(Essential poets series ; 168)
ISBN 978-1-55071-308-4
I. Title. II. Series: Essential poets series ; 168
PS8605.H453S54 2009   C811'.6   C2009-906144-9

Contents

FOR STEVE

To the Woman Whose Notebook I Found in the Puces de Vanves

I have your book – your recipes
copied in blue ink,
kept to ruled lines,
the pages brown- and brittle-edged,
aged...
        (or were they singed?)
a flame leaping in your kitchen

I see where you dipped
your pen, letters paling
      mélanger, et pétrir
                then
taking up again, freshly dark
      jusqu'à...

You wrote the title in English –
      Steak and Kidney Pudding.
Were you homesick?
Was it strange, clothing in French names
those familiar motions – mix, and knead

Or were you brimful of optimism,
determined on your new life,
sitting erect as any French wife
in a sunny window,
pen poised to strike the spelling of *pétrir*?

Between the pages, chance-saved clues:
an envelope addressed Bayonne;
a card, "with love, from Auntie Phil,"
a ticket, 1942.

The recipes – for you? a friend? a mother-in-law?
Is it her hand that alternates
in strong forward-tilted strokes
with your round and sturdy backhand?
Did you share a kitchen?
Could you hold your own?
At the sink, hands plunged
in soap- and grease-filmed water,
were you content? Consumed
with irritation? Did you notice
rain as it slid down the window?

I want – for even a moment – to see you clearly,
be you, in your skin,
and in leaving my own,
feel the world's
wide wind blowing through
the time between us.

Fragility

We barred the Windows and the Doors
As from an emerald Ghost –
The Doom's electric Moccasin
That very instant passed

"There came a Wind like a Bugle"
Emily Dickinson

Had we known, we might
have taken better care.
Had we considered fragility,
fidelity, the importance of shelter,
we might have built our house
more prudently – thought of storm panes,
weather stripping. Then at least
we could have said, later –
as if to prove we couldn't have done more –
We barred the Windows and the Doors

Though in those soft green days,
it would have seemed foolish as Noah
hammering with no cloud in sight.
The lush summers were simply
the world set right,
and we – freed into happiness –
welcomed it whole, unseamed,
delighted in warm winds' messages,
now-and-then whispered lusts,
As from an Emerald Ghost

How was it we thought
no misstep we made (so casually)
could alter what we had?
Say we were young, had little sense.
Say we forgot to shut the windows,
bolt the door – that even with locks,
a restless presence
would have roamed our rooms:
For where would we find
The Doom's electric Moccasin

but on our own feet, still unsettled,
given to swerves and meanders,
charged by currents still
coursing through us unconsidered,
seeking their own way.
When, finally, we turned
to make repairs, we found,
too late, the chimney crumbled,
roof half-gone, the moment missed:
That very instant, passed.

Transoms

Across quiet back lawns, lighted windows,
		golden, amber, ivory
squares of silk in mat black night,

patterned with shadow-lace of leaves,
		the thickened darkness
a branch's curve, a slanted bole,

or, with the calm geometry of transoms
		and mullions,
soft light quilted into squares;

the straight lines of a porch rail,
		balusters,
a glow sifted into even stripes.

Here, a pine bough droops,
		brushed design
against a fall of honeyed satin,

and there – a calligraphy of twigs
		complicatedly clear
as the unfolding of dream.

In the Whispering Hall

At the abbey of La Chaise-Dieu in the Auvergne

They say lepers made confession here,
and cowled monks,
standing back to back across the room's diagonal,
spoke to stone.
Whispers carry upward,
the corner gradually relinquishes
its sharp-angled identity,
merging into a vault
where breath slips
across the creaseless centre
over an imperceptible edge
funneled in the other's ear.

"The room's proportions..." I enthuse,
"...an eye to beauty..."
"Chilly," you disparage,
"in these old stone places."

At odds all trip, we choose stances:
mine, appreciation, yours,
solid practicality.
It seems possible we could switch,
if that were more convenient, words
the mere surface of stubborn mother-
daughter battle. Habitual.

We are not at peace together
looking at paint like patterned ribbon
high on walls; down at breath level,
corners stained and chipped
from years of exhaled acids
as murmurs mounted the domed vault.

We try it too,
backs turned, apart in corners,
the softest whisper:
"Can you hear me?"
"Yes."

How strange, this momentary intimacy,
as when I was a child
your voice dropped pure into my ear,
so that I wonder, afterwards,
if the old monks weren't right, dividing
soul from flesh –
the stubborn competition of our wills
a habit locked in cells,
our spirits capable of love.

Family Furniture

"Some Sundays," my sister-in-law says,
"we spend the whole day
trying to rearrange the room.
That heavy, old buffet –
I wish we didn't have it."

"I think it's beautiful," I answer.

Carved flowers wreathed with slender stems.
Brass pulls – cool dusted
hollows of the small spoons.

Inside the drawer, gold damask,
blue-bordered white linens handed down,
with long-leaved table and buffet,
from my father's childhood home.
Folded in tissue they whispered
city, elegance, sun spilling
over my grandmother's parquet floor –
brought its luster
to our drafty small-town house.

The gleaming mahogany told us,
each Sunday, that we were happy,
chosen, eating together
from our best china. Even
in the grey times, when my father
ate without speaking,
while my mother and brothers and I
worked at conversation,
walling silence behind words –
even then, food gone cold,

lumpy on my plate,
the polished buffet insisted
this was aberration, not
our lives.

"You take it, then," my nephew says –
half joke, half challenge.
"You'd trade?" his mother asks.
"Your dining room for ours?"

I nod, imagine it
for the moment it takes
to catch my lie –
our dining room, days away
in a distant city, where
I've chosen a table and sideboard
of pale birchwood, surfaces
planed smooth,
and in the drawers are placemats,
not linens long enough
to drape a childhood's ghost.

Making Bread Pudding in Paris

I imagined something like a séance,
    small kitchen,
        large window,
            late afternoon's low light

Ceremoniously
    I'd open your notebook,
        found at a windy-morning flea market,
            black-bound, filled with recipes in fading ink

Slowly,
    turning the page mid-sentence
        (as you must have done)
            I'd retrieve your Method, assemble
                butter, bread, 1 pint of milk, sultanas –
                range them neatly on the counter
                a reception line

While I sliced and buttered,
    beat eggs with sugar, paused
        to watch the neighbour's window-framed cat
        at his evening game, batting a cord,

I'd hold in mind's eye your blue-inked backhand,
    invite your ghost to dance once-familiar
        motions, layer, sprinkle,
            bend to oven

You'd come, into this simple room
    in a strange country, unlittered
        with crumbs of busyness,
            crusts of old strivings

The quiet would take your faint impress
    like fine, pliant clay.
      Finding your hand,
         careful not to grip too hard,
            I'd step out of my skin,

bent, reading
    mix in the milk and pour gently over the bread
      gently
         a glimpse in a word
            who you might have been.

Old Letters

My father's P's and D's
wide-looped in his exuberance
or close-huddled
when his spirit failed

my uncle's spider-small slant,
webbed secrets told to a brother –
I've got to get this off my chest...

That bent "r" in my grandmother's
straight-shouldered typing

my mother's sturdy backhand –
each letter leaning on the one before,
the first on air

my own leggy scrawl at ten,
careful cursive at twenty:

I thought a pattern would show clear through
the box hauled from the closet,
and I'd see the way a man in a balloon
reads a lake deep to the bottom

but I could only follow from one season
to the next, caught up in
swirls, downstrokes, the old
longing for a future
with everything made right,

and finally,
I replaced the box in the far dark
behind shoes and coats,
                              turned
to fix a meal, as my mother
would on any of those days
when she wrote her news,
and looked out at a mottled sky
the way my father would,
to note the passing weather.

Ritual

All summer I've watered your maple sapling,
spindly bole in a new-mounded collar of earth.
I plant puddled footprints at the river's edge,
squat to fill a bucket, scatter minnows
with my small commotion, then, arm out for balance,
climb the bank through brush and waist-high grasses.

In sunny back and forth a stem of purple loosestrife
catches my thought ... or the maple's crown
bent toward the river. Grasses mat underfoot.
At the tree's base, tilting the bucket, I watch soil
darken, each time a wider ring. Dog-walkers
pass, mallards on the slow current

you walked by, gauging the river's depth,
scanning the banks' tall thickets of weeds.
Once you saw a great blue heron.
Even when darkness branched in you, pushing shoots
into thoughts, you were eased seeing an oak in a field,
clouds of birds settling their beating wings.

Belatedly I've chosen a memorial, this tree muscled
into spring ground by a city crew. *Soak it*,
they said, *enough so water stands in the dirt saucer.*
I hadn't counted on that – weekly ritual of reeds
and river, lift or droop of leaves.
Once, the current I stirred drew a crayfish

from under its rock. My brother saw a beetle
and knew it was you, visiting, with an iridescent back.
I couldn't accept such solace, your death like roots
buried in me, closed off, tears sealed up
with questions that cling like bindweed.
I didn't ask them as I crossed the sun-baked ground

between the river and the maple's fresh-turned loam.
But I've felt an ease in my physical self,
something soothed by hours among wild phlox
and the alder brush leaving fine scratches on my knees
while my arm grew stronger with the sloshing pail,
a ring of grass greened round your tree.

Step back

as he would have, from the easel in his garden

> dark rain
> > of willow leaves
>
> and shadow

> the bridge an arc
> brown teal chartreuse melt
> into the fall of willow green

squint –   he was seventy-eight

> light limned through thin
> > > foliage
> > lime azure gold

> dark swirls
> thicket the far bank

in the foreground
> a leaning
> > toward a space of sun

> beneath the curve of bridge above
> watery branches falling up to meet it

look through eyelashes –   he saw through cataracts

> past the leafy spill   water
> begins to shimmer

pink lilies glow

until the screen of leaves
          ·and what shone beyond

     are one green gold dark
                         thinning

          traces of light float

We Were Here

My neighbour is pissing
in his backyard again. He can't know
he's been observed – that I've happened
to look out a window just as he
unzipped his fly in a corner
masked by cedar hedge, near the brick patio
he set last summer, and the shed
he started three years ago –
blue tarp still draped over the top.
This hasn't been his habit
until recently – I'm often at my desk
and would have noticed, looking out
at prowling cats and the sway of leaves.

He and his wife are separating.
Their two young boys, who raced and shouted
and jumped their junior bikes over
dirt my neighbour hilled up by the drive,
appear only occasionally now on weekends.
Yesterday, a crew arrived to strip
old shingles and replace the roof.
The house will soon go up for sale, I think,
and wonder if his pissing
is an impulse (though it could be simply
that the bathroom is being repaired) to mark
this place he's lived for seven years:

The way we chalk on ruined walls,
carve names into desks and trees – notes
to the old gods in wood and stone:
Remember us. We were here.

Gauges

I haven't seen you for two weeks, which is not
so very long, really, and we've been apart
that much and more before in years of marriage –
often alone together, over newspapers and porridge,

but today – because it's midsummer, the leaves
poised on an edge of sun and stillness, so green
they make me think of red, or because when you called
last night you asked me, had our zinnias grown tall,

whatever reason – when I boarded the plane
and waited, gazing into the cockpit while the line
bumped through the narrow aisle, each gauge,
every knob and lever, the compass and altimeter ranged
in their panel, all were meant to know
just one purpose: to carry me to you.

The Gâtine

1
Waking

Land of ancient pastures and soft rain,
magpies nested in pale poplar trees,
stone houses, hedgerows lush with blackberries
I picked that fall along the muddy lane,
sure that I'd found, here, my way back again
to nature: still that unchanged self, peace
embraced in ageless mysteries;
I'd live enfolded in this green-wound skein.
But winter mornings, wakened in damp chill,
nagged through fog by magpie scold,
I shivered, shrugged quilts close, huddled until,
hungry for breakfast, finally I rolled
the bedclothes back and stepped – an act of will –
on stone, sense-shocking, adamant, and cold.

2
Madame Moreau

On stone, pervasive, adamant, and cold,
my neighbours in the hamlet made their way:
Worn flagstones paved the yards; and under hay
slow-ripened in the fields, a bedrock fold
of granite chilled spring ground and kept on hold
the growing season so that earth must stay
as pasture – not one vineyard, no display
of golden wheat: a stubborn land, cajoled,
where mornings, with her goats, Madame Moreau
led out along the forest road. The gate
swung free, its latch end never sagging low,
lifted by wire and pole, and she, pole-straight,
walked through, right-angled to the earth, as though
stone held erect her slender human weight.

3
Bending

Stone held erect their slender human weight –
farmers and wives with lifted heads, straight-spined,
but supple too: they stooped each night to find
goats' teats, and bent in spring to separate
wet twin-birthed lambs, to rake, or sweep a grate,
clear dead stalks, seed the garden. When wind
tore off a shed roof, they calmly inclined
their thoughts to tools, ladder, layered slate.
They bowed to season's task and accident,
but bent, too, gathering gifts: firm *marrons*
that littered lanes in fall, or, in ferment
of forest leaves, wild *cêpes*; and when sun shone
in March, in still-cool air – soft colour and scent
of *marguerites* scattered through grass, wind-sown.

4
Weather

White *marguerites* scattered in grass, wind-sown,
pebbles, mice, even these small things near ground
were buffeted. Sheep huddled, wild cats crouched
close to walls, tall poplars' wind-lashed crowns
bowed in low arcs when the westerlies, grown
powerful over ocean, sweeping round
the globe, stormed inland. Hard-flung rain drowned
fields, pounded furrows under wind's harsh drone.
Their lives suffused with weather, men used it
as they could – got from downed branches a store
of firewood, picked up windfalls that lay hid
in grass, and, on clear-blown days every door
and window was thrown open to admit
sharp wind, scour out the damp, sweep each floor.

5
Darkness

Windows, opened to let wind sweep each floor,
at night were shuttered, shelter. From outside,
dark sifted under doors – whisper of wide-
winged blackness settled into shrubs in pores
of stones. Sentinel poplars, no more
separate branched shapes, were one glide
of shadow: daytime's sharp divide
of form from form, and time from time before,
blurred. Night seeped where wind had swept,
soft current that mingled experience
of neighbour, ancestor, of cats who crept
beneath night-soaked hedges, and the immense
dark-folded land, horizonless. Men slept –
eased by night's dark beneficence.

6
Turning

Eased round, turned from night's dark beneficence
through dawn and cloudy morning toward bright noon,
into the clarity of work and sun
the fields revolved, and each day's violence
or peace was subsumed in a silent sense
of circling: day, month, season – yearly tune
of strident magpies nesting, then soon, dun
leaves underfoot, drab winter's imminence.
Along the forest road in that curved time,
contented in the days' routine – unrushed pace
of an early walk, coffee and the climb
up attic stairs to write, I felt this place
a ring of endless ripples, the clock's chime
a skipping stone; eternal cycles, grace.

7
Calm

Earth's hard cold stone, eternal cycles, grace –
I read these in the book of my sojourn;
living there – yet, not – knowing I'd return
to this other life; free in thoughts to trace
the ancient landscape's features – though what face
the land wore for my neighbours, bound to earn
a whole life with sensible concern
for daily tasks and detail's constant chase,
I couldn't know. Some must have liked it less,
some more, like any home. Still, it was plain
they wouldn't trade their hard life's peacefulness:
C'est calme ici, they said – like a refrain
that calms me now, as I remember, yes,
it was a land of pastures and soft rain.

Quilting for a First Husband

Buckling to the urge
to make something beautiful – or useful –
from clothes far back in my closet,
I hoist my scissors

to iridescent taffeta, shimmer
of hopeful high school parties,
packed and unpacked through
college, our marriage, its ending,
new beginnings with others.

Jeans frayed thin
that backpack summer after you left.
Old hiking shirt,
bold day-glo miniskirt.
All unworn for years, except

that now and then I wear them
in my thoughts,
a college girl in black chiffon,
young bride in white brocade,
old selves kept
on hangers, clothes I couldn't
bear to give away, though they claim
too much space.

At last I cut – wincing –
taffeta and faded jeans.
Once begun I see how I can stitch
silk and denim to gaudy polyester,
pull mingled colors over me
for warmth, let pattern
entertain my eye.

I snip and plan a Roman stripe,
prints paired with plains.
But at the white brocade
I stick, can't cut
the yellowed roses still raised
like young yearning
toward some perfect beauty.
I want it whole,
intact, the way I keep your image
so that I can swim back to it
in dream.

Foolish, isn't it? You're not
an image. The yellowed dress
is useless.

Buttons

In her effort to empty the house
my mother has given away the box of buttons –
pearlescent plastic, leather toggles,
small, shanked silver balls
and rounds of bone, saved
from worn-out sweaters, or still
threaded to paste-board cards –
the dress they were meant for
never made, or made another way.

When we'd open the box in the attic,
it would tumble color,
cool weight to palm
and sift through fingers, familiar,
pleasing coppery glimmer-
ghost of a party dress,
faintly troubling bits of thread
like phantom griefs half-unraveled,
twisted through holes.

When my mother said she'd given
the buttons to her friend, a crafter,
I imagined them lighter,
a weight fallen from discs and knobs
that now will make jewelry, pillow tufts,
small wheels or eyes.

          In the attic,
sunlight strikes the empty shelf,
the air is thinner.

Like a House by Magritte

Late on a winter Sunday and the sky,
when I drop my book in my lap,
is indigo, the trees' twiggy filigree

a pattern my fingers could trace,
branches to forks to sprigs
to buds – the world,

I decide,
logically arranged,

until my eye drifts,

to roofs,
to the house down the block
with half-finished new rooms,

and silhouette-black branches
in the tall blue windows –
a house filled with sky,

like a house by Magritte.
And now, my jug-shaped table lamp
has slipped, with its oval of light,

through the window and storm pane,
floating into night,
the silver shade a glassy ghost,

diaphanous among rooftops and trees.

Sighting

"Well," she said at breakfast,
musing on a chance remark,
"I wouldn't want to be an eagle.
Maybe a goldfinch.
There's always lots of them together
around the thistle seed."

And now at this reception
I see her with a plate of chocolate cake,
talking to a woman she's only just met.
Her lined face is luminous:
bright as a flash of gold
that catches your eye at the edge
of a field, where thistles plume
softly in the wind.

What was it I wanted her to be
all those years? Thoughtful robin,
listener, head tilted to the grass?
Dove, a steady reassurance of murmurs?
Loon, lover and singer of solitude?

Never mind.
She nods and smiles, waves hellos
in this pavilion full of late summer light.

Trespass

The ones my mother read
she found in my desk; she would have had
to open it, search through small drawers
and cubbies, where I closed them
out of reach: They weren't hers. The kissing
and touching those letters remembered
were not for her touch. "I know,"
she said triumphantly afterwards,
"what went on." For years I held
and hated that moment,
her stern gloating, like a claw.

Now, out of the blue,
over wine and duck, my visiting younger brother,
so close growing up I thought us
twins, says to the table at large –
to his wife and my husband – "You know,
in high school I got letters from a girl in Tomahawk.
I hid them in my Bible, and Sue found them.
She *found* them." A fine
accusing edge in his voice.

I'm stung, stunned, though the moment
passes, the old grudged hurt
slipped with conscious or unconscious cunning
into conversation's flow. I have
no memory of the letters, or the girl,
and want to plead:
It was only
a small thing, wasn't it?

Brueghel's Winter

Three hunters trudge home through snow,
trailed by rib-thin hounds,
one skinny fox slung
on a pole over the tall man's back.

He bends into his step,
the brim of his dark hat tilted
toward the slope which drops
to a village,
               its roofs
smoothed into the broad flatness
of the valley, church spire
dwarfed against tree-dotted fields
and distant crags
                    unremarked by the hunters
in stained jerkins, their sturdy
calves round as winter-bare tree trunks
that rise from the hillside, lifting
branches and birds.

                  One swoops, wings
wide above ponds and skaters, tree-lined roads,
far fields, almost escaping –

                      in the painted moment,
gravity slumps the tired hounds,
slopes the snow-drenched earth back to itself.

Hush

Complicit in the abandon of late day sleep,
the cat pressed behind my knees,
and I woke at dusk, the windowed sky
thick with the pink diffusion of city light.
Tree limbs, bulky and ridged with snow,
or scribbled fine above rooftops, waited
for a clock to tick again.

                When I was a girl,
this hush came, sometimes, late on a winter Saturday.
My brother and I sat on a radiator and watched cars,
the orange Phillips 66 sign across the highway,
                                  that border
between now and all that had yet to happen,
waiting for us beyond the motionless branches.

Return

North from the airport, dark highway,
headlights flare pale into ghostly trees.

We startle animals, point them out
to each other, my sister and I:

red-tinged buck, poised to flee,
white cat stone-still on the gravel shoulder.

Fox nose and tail, flowing grey streak –
if we could fix his shape, stop time...

"...by morning. We've rented a car,"
I'd said to our mother over anxious long distance.

We thought we knew every bend in the dark, the way
home, always-known litany of small-town names

but we miss a turn. "Where is Amery? Turtle Lake?"
On a neon island, lights dim. We rap on glass.

The boy cleaning up gives courteous directions.
From the car, I look back,

I want to arrest his motion, but he pushes his mop –
the world going about its ordinary business.

Deep in night we slip from hills
onto the lake's ancient bed, almost there,

and my sister honors family ritual:
"We have to watch for the tall white pine.

It should still be there.
Right at Nine Mile Corner."

Storm

She was nowhere, between there and here,
sailing six lanes of concrete,
signposts bobbing like flotsam,
her mind keeling along yellow lines
in a monotony of sunlight.

A song on the radio –
you know the one,
by Schubert, or John and Paul,
or Mahler. It blew in
unexpected, rousing
what used to rise
from sweet dark tones,
something tall and golden,
some life she'd meant to live.
Passing semis startled her
with their swift, heavy purpose,
she drove buffeted
by gusts of regret,
each green/white exit now
some turn she might
have missed, tires keening
on the highway for time
slipped by

                    until
she reached the outskirts
of the city she called home,
where streets came out to meet her
filled with dailiness –

the turn to a friend's house,
entrance to a garden store,
laneway behind a library
lulled her
into a safe harbour,
whispered, enough.

At the St. Cloud Veterans' Hospital

for my father

You stood beside the window, hands
clamped into fists – hands you'd
bloodied, pounding –
your knuckles taut and
shiny, scabbed,
head bowed and shoulders
hunched as if you'd fold into yourself
and disappear.

On your bedside stand, a paper cup
for pills
you held beneath your tongue
and spat
out when the nurses left.

Your pants were loose,
belt high around your waist
like an old man's,
and when I hugged you
you were stiff, though feeble as a doll,
and I wanted to pound
your thin shoulder blades, and shout,
"Hug me back, hug me back."

"I guess I could show you around."
Your voice thin, resigned.
You signed out meekly
while the nurse watched.

"He's such a gentleman," she said, as if you
weren't there.
She stood, unlocked the ward.

Through dim halls,
down stairs, through heavy doors,
round corners where gaunt men
with bathrobes, whiskers, spittle, canes,
sat mumbling.
"Not you
here!" I thought, and wondered at
how surely you found your way,
as if you'd prowled
each corridor,
marked paths down
in your secret, curious mind.

"We swim in here," you said.
The pool was empty, cracked,
walls high, close, windowless.
"They're fixing it, we couldn't
swim this week."
The smell of chlorine lingered in the air.

You tried the craft room door.
A box marked with your name
held printed pictures, colored
carefully within the lines.
"Some people make leather belts," you said,
"but I've
just done these."
A bowl of fruit.
A winter forest scene. "They only
have two greens," you frowned, "and here –
they should have drawn a space, for snow

on branches."
The hovering smell of grease,
men waiting near
smudged swinging doors for lunch.
A boy in stained white trousers took my pass;
he counted you, one click
on the metal cylinder in his palm.

You ate salmon loaf, peas, orange jello, thick dry
cake, deliberate bites,
and I watched,
knowing I'd report: "He ate
today. He might be getting better."

I had a plan.
I got a pass
so we could walk the grounds.
How could you heal indoors,
you who tramped so many fields
with farmers, surveyed
their ditches and woodlots.
They kept you in now, since
you'd spent a night beneath a tree in cold,
continuous rain.

Today was sunny, and I knew
to ask the names of trees,
to draw you out –
wasn't I your oldest daughter,
the one you taught
MAD HORSE for Maple, Ash,
Dogwood, Horsechestnut, all
the trees with opposite branching.
"That's Norway spruce," you answered.

"That's red oak; white oak
has deeper lobes."
I thought if I could only be here
every day
to talk to you about trees
you'd be all right.

"Let's get lemonade in the canteen," I said,
"or coffee? or some pie?"
You sat across the booth and watched,
not hungry, gone silent again,
and I, panicked, pushed with questions while a fan,
blades clogged with greasy dust,
turned slowly in the wall.
"What will you do tomorrow?
When do you think they'll fix the pool? Do you
remember the time we climbed Old Baldy
and saw the ovenbird?"

You nodded, frowning.
My sentences gave out.
All that was left,
before we said goodbye:
to sit with you
quietly
and let you be
as you would be.

Dragon

Along the river path, beyond the bend
where mallards swim in wind-scuffed water,
and just before a dirt track
short-cuts up the hill – someone
has carved a dragon.

Yellow eyes, black snout, red maw,
eight jagged teeth below and eight above,
he peers over the bank from his crouch
among alder shoots, grey ghosts of leaves,
clumps of crab-grass limp in the November air.
His tail's down by the water, near pebbled
styrofoam, blue plastic
washed up in shriveled white grass...
and a gnawed stump, red-rimmed
where the artist cleaned his brush:

This fire-breathing creature
was rough-barked willow until
someone, anonymous
as the beavers that felled it,
hacked out a furrowed forehead,
brushed black along the bark for scales,
added red nostrils, and left him
to grin at us, out of leaves and grass.

Caribou for Brass Players

Caribou. Running
gracefully across tundra.
Mucky channels between tussocks.
The knots of grass slippery,
tilted, betray the foot
unless you step
precisely.

Loping over rough
ground, he lifts
his rack of antlers – heavy
bone sculpture
of curves and prongs
balanced on his head.

Sturdy haunches,
supple back,
sharp horn hooves all
at the service of this
ornament.

As if someone would sprint, carrying
a heavy silver platter engraved
with scrolls and roses just
to decorate
the low wide sweep of plain.

As if someone would
practice
a trombone or French horn
every day long tones
and scales, just
to make a Bruckner symphony
soar.

Once More With Feeling

Ever since morning he's hummed
tunes he used to play – *Misty, Body and Soul*.
When he went to Uptown Music to buy guitar strings
for his son, he found the same scuffed sheet music,
guitars crammed in a narrow aisle – the place
unchanged from back when he lugged a tenor sax
to weekly lessons. Even the guy
at the cash looked right – grey curly hair,
harried patience – though of course
it had to be someone else.
He asked when he paid for the strings:
Would it have been your dad who taught me?

Matted plush when he opened the case.
Spit in old brass.
Woolly underside of the neck strap.
      He'd had a pretty good sound –
    more Hawkins than Coltrane.
Always a trumpet or a flute next door,
commotion in the hall. The rough cough
that prefaced some correction
drove him half-crazy: he'd wanted
the music whole, the bell-
shaped fullness of it, part of him
heavy with disappointment every time
the old guy sliced it into
dotted eighths and sixteenths,
slurs and staccatos. Something
broken in the knowing.

Still, as he hums those smooth, sweet tunes
through the afternoon he feels
how they're part of him, articulated
in muscle and lungs.

                    Glad
for every melody that's his, wondering
what songs will stay with his son,
he fingers the guitar strings in his pocket,
their coiled silk and metal.

The Poet at Métro Alésia

"...un petit poème, monsieur..."
Mornings in the Métro, his overture
echoed up stairs. In worn
shoes, a decent coat, wan-
faced, he chanted, *un cri de coeur* –

I thought, finding everywhere,
even in pigeons' plaintive murmur,
soulful poems. I bought one –
                    un petit poème.

Lines of his? I asked. *"Bien sûr."*
Lines of shipwreck, what we endure –
but from Victor Hugo's romantic pen!
Typed, sold for a few *francs*
to ease – like the pigeons' – a plainer hunger:
                    un petit poème.

Cardamom

Un petit poème

Wild phlox along our jogging path smells sweet –
and look – a pair of monarchs in the sun.
I've heard that butterflies taste with their feet.

Our day is planned. We both have lists complete
with weekend chores and errands to be done
while phlox, along this river path, waves sweetly

its spiced scent drawn out in drowsy heat:
vanilla underlain with cardamom
invites shy butterflies to feast.

Groceries, laundry, grass to mow: a suite
of tasks – we said today's for work, not fun,
but oh, these wild phlox by the path entreat,

and make me think it wouldn't hurt to cheat
our lists, taste this day before it's gone.
We can match the butterfly's fine feat,

savor with skin when our warm bodies meet.
I'll tease you with a kiss when I get home
to stop and smell the blossoms while they're sweet,
taste, like the butterflies, entwining feet.

Intimacy

His arm knows the ladle
    heft of three-fourths full,
        rotation of radius
            and ulna that tips
                thin crêpe batter over lip

Wrist knows the spreader,
    runs the rhythm of a swivel
        overhand, underhand, loose-held
            handle, wood blade, batter
                smoothed in a circle

Knee knows the depth of bend
    to fridge, shoulder
        the height of shelved towels,
            hand the weight of cheese,
                trajectory of salt

Index finger knows the spatula –
    stretched against each other
        they pat, fold, flip the crêpe,
            caress and furl it,
                slip a smooth withdrawal

Flame knows his eye,
    as tilted head gauges
        orange flare, blue fire,
            while on the grill, browned edges
            of the next crêpe,
                    the next

Scene with Blue Fruit Bowl
and Orange

We've cleared away the crusts
this Sunday noon after
our morning bodies tangled
and rocked against each other.

Now our table is strewn
with your music scores,
my open newspaper,
the fruit bowl holding an orange.

You're leafing through
illustrated cowboy songs,
checking the words to tunes
in a suite for band.

My paper brushes the blue bowl –
the orange, peeled,
translucent segments
in the slant of sun.

"The Railroad Corral!"
Your face lights, memory
jarred: railway stockyards
in Clovis, New Mexico.

"I used to ride there
on my Whizzer bike," you tell me.
"They have a sweetish smell.
Not unpleasant."

And that whiff, not unpleasant,
bawling cattle, summer dust,
the wind in your face
as you motor on your Whizzer

comes in through my open pores,
while we look together at the picture,
our table cleared of crusts,
strewn with newspaper and scores.

Draperies Relaxed in Their Folds

We hadn't been gone long –
only the half hour it took
to reach the edge of town,
remember a forgotten passport,
return in a rush.
When I entered the vestibule
the house had already composed itself,
calm as a hostess who sits down
to read the paper after
visitors have left.

The curtains, relaxed in their folds,
had become more nearly the blue cloth
they were before we sewed them;
the wooden table recalled
not our meals, but straight maple
planed to show a sinuous grain;
the vase, free of last week's flowers,
settled into squat roundness.

How quickly and with what relief
they abandoned our frets and pleasures.
They seemed startled by my return,
as if they weren't expecting
to reveal that they had only
lent themselves to us,
how the blue fabric would brush
the window sill when we were gone.

Bay Window

Now... you say, *now it's the places.*
Do you remember the bay window in Phillips?
That big sunny window...

It was where you ironed.
Plunk and glide,
half-rank smell of cheap starched cotton.

I did my thinking then, you told me once
as we folded tumble-dry clothes
and remembered wringers and clothespins:

steam fizzling over a collar,
sunlight, begonias on the sill...
      which dress?   and how
             to wear your hair...
cuff, sleeve, span of thin grass
and the maple's sprawled shadow
      ...or what had she meant
      by that, exactly...

Mondays, shirts snap on the backyard line.
In the air, a tang of whey,
the dust-and-chicken smell
from Flambeau Feeds.
          Their semi-trailer
parked across the highway on new gravel,
its red bulk looming before the lake,
a fight you lost;
though something was salvaged, new
grass for picnickers farther down.

                    You never meant
to live in a small Wisconsin town – *a city girl* –
but settled in, got involved,

                    and on Fridays,
out across the lake at Dobshutz',
you polka and schottish,
Jim the best dancer in your crowd.
His mood lifts then,
you come home a little tipsy,
laugh and whisper *Don't wake the kids*,
and it's like being young together
in Minneapolis again, at the University...

    I did my thinking then...
the maple spills its shade
as you iron, and the place
absorbs your rhythms,
knows your step.

I'd give it back to you if I could –
the sidewalk elms,
the bare spot on the lawn,
the feed truck – a mirror, map,
the bay window
inscribed with who you were.

African Music

for Adelia Hultgren Jones

Her cheek still warm when I arrived.

Smell of menthol, unguent, undertone of urine.

Bruises blacken the back of her hand
where she scratched deep,
wedding band loose, now simply
a golden round object.
The white down of her hair almost too fine
to feel between fingertips.
Forehead wrinkles cut by furrows,
only below the faint widow's peak
smooth skin soft as an infant's.

    At death, what spirits abandon bone?

Was there an infant, cradle-lulled,
tomboy balanced barefoot on barbed wire,
young teacher with pupils in a blizzard, huddled?

    Had these slipped away long since,
    molted selves,
    or were they breathed out
    into the room's dense sunlight?

Aged, blind, her lap-robe smoothed
by the young black aide who wheels her chair,
tells her she's lookin' fine today,
in his deep lilting tones.

She'd yelled and yelled
the night before, "African music!
I want African music!"
until her voice was gone,
not even a whisper.

The Church in Riez, Provence

Rounded as an apple
or a womb, the low nave
curved above me bends
back to earth.

Dim pupil-widening light.
Saints appear at pillars,
secrets carved in folds of robes.

Their hems brushed sand and stone.
They walked where psalms lay
tangled deep with roots,
and hooked them out
with crook-neck staves or drew them
down from night blue sky,
the blue behind the altar.

If I came every day
to this church,
dark and cool,
a step away from the square
with sun and sycamores
and dust and tourists' cars,

would I fathom
the curve of the vault,
the depth of the blue?
Would old mysteries
seep through stone-slab floors
into my feet?

Pray Do Not Touch

Among dim statues
this deep, round vessel's
marbled weight – sculpted
basin of a cloister fountain,
from *Saint-Michel-de-Grandmont*.

The curved rim is fingered
smooth above carved columns,
leafy capitals – ornament
that must have mirrored
the arcade of an open court

where water trickled
from the stone fountain,
a kind of constant weather,
days and seasons absorbed
into the heavy bowl.

Prière de ne pas toucher:
Impossible, almost,
not to disobey, rub
the worn lip...
What would be the harm?

And here's a fat fly,
almost brushing marble
with her lustrous abdomen
as she threads a path
into the *vasque's* round depth.

Exempt from rules, she extends
a curious leg, probes
the pocked surface,
translucent wings stilled.
How lightly, with what gentle

measure of its depths and heights
she touches this solid vessel
that holds, like yellowed maps,
the sense of lost time.
Press too hard,

and patterned potsherds
are only clay,
a basin simply marble,
the dreams they whispered
lost to imagining.

Clever fly. I'll learn
from you, touch this rim
so softly – one light brush –
and listen for the water's
quiet splash.

Eve's Fruit

Cybèle, *Leratess*, smooth
peels freckled, blushing
as if you stroked
round flesh, roused
streaks of color

Monidel, faint anise
teasing tongue, *Rubinette*,
unexpected, remembered
otherness of your breath
deep-bitten, tart
sweet, mingled mouth
tongue teeth touch

Jubilé, Mars-red,
moon-round, palm-glided
carmine globe
shaped to your hand

Boskoop, rude welcome, *Cox
Orange*, cleft and stem, musky
rough bronze of lichen,
mushroom, tuber selves, earth-hid

Clochard, fallen wanton, split
in wet roadside grass,
Chantecler, *Cox Fiesta*,

Calville,
quince-grooved
bump
knob
fissure, deep
secreted cotyledon
hypocotyl
raphe
hilum
burst in ancient orchard
sprung seed

Pelt me with apples.
Apple me.

Chardin's Apple

How did he hold that apple
so sharply in heart's eye,
layering paint until peel gleamed,
bulged, hid flesh, stem, seeds?

Above, a limp-necked partridge,
stiff-limbed hare, its sunken
eye a dull brown answer
to the apple's swelling red.

Below, a cat, pink nose
and pointed ears alert, head
turned, neck stretched, looking –
more curious, still, than greedy –

at the lolling head, splayed
wings, jut of forepaws,
white belly fur still soft
as his own, death's odd

small difference. Partridge
and hare just that side,
the apple this side,
its life located, held

in view, potent, miraculous.
I'd never seen how fine before –
thin wavering line –
mingled breath and death.

Notes

The Puces de Vanves is a flea market in Paris.

"Step back" is after Claude Monet's *Le Pont Japonais, 1918.*

The Gâtine is a region in west central France, near Poitiers.

"Brueghel's Winter" is after *Hunters in the Snow* by Pieter Brueghel the Elder.

"Chardin's Apple" is after *Un chat guettant une perdrix et un lievre morts* ("A cat looking intently at a dead partridge and hare") by Jean-Baptiste-Siméon Chardin.

Acknowledgements

Grateful acknowledgement is made to the editors of the following journals, where some of these poems, often in earlier versions, first appeared: *Agenda, The Antigonish Review, Chiron Review, Contemporary Verse 2, Descant, The Fiddlehead, The New Quarterly, Pagitica, Rhythm Poetry Magazine, Tears in the Fence,* and *Upstairs at Duroc.* Thanks, too, to Steve Chenette for his unfailing support and perceptive readings of my work; A.F. Moritz for his generous guidance in classes at St. Michael's College; Bruce Meyer, guru of formal verse; Paris poet friends Barbara Beck, Jennifer Dick, and George Vance; Allan Briesmaster, for always valued advice; members of the Art Bar poetry group; staff and participants in the 2004 Wired Writing Program at the Banff Centre, particularly Sue Wheeler; Molly Peacock, for her literary acumen; Maureen Scott Harris, Ruth Roach Pierson, Patty Rivera, Julie Roorda, and Norma Rowen for shared poems, Pro Secco, and laughter; the Warren Wilson writing community for continuing support, conversation, and inspiration; Elana Wolff for her insightful editing of the manuscript; and Antonio D'Alfonso of Guernica Editions, for his dedicated work in publishing.

In *Slender Human Weight*, Sue Chenette explores a world both familiar and mysterious. She finds, in her mother's attic, in the French countryside, or her own home, the richness of physical objects as they embody what is felt, dreamed, longed for, and remembered.

"Sue Chenette's poems have that rare quality of being lit from within. Reading them is like discovering someone dancing, perfectly poised, alone in a room. Chenette offers us privileged glimpses into interior life, not merely described, but lived. It is curious that we speak of being graceful in quite a different context than being in a state of grace, but Chenette's poetry, burnished, delicate, but sturdy, shows us both. Lucid, yet full of the mystery of complex adult emotions, *Slender Human Weight* is alluring and wise." — Molly Peacock

"Sue Chenette's poems are gorgeously precise, writing a "careful cursive" through the past, putting memories in their place. *Slender Human Weight* is full of the most elegant ghostings, as if Chenette herself were the life force, her sights on everything, from fruit bowls to faith, from buttons to full-blown love." — Barry Dempster

Sue Chenette is the author of three chapbooks: *The Time Between Us*, *A Transport of Grief*, and *Solitude in Cloud and Sun*. *Slender Human Weight* is her first full length collection. The author lives in Toronto.

Recycled
Supporting responsible use
of forest resources
www.fsc.org Cert no. SGS-COC-2624
© 1996 Forest Stewardship Council

FSC

Printed in November 2009
at Gauvin Press,
Gatineau, Québec